WRITTEN & ILLUSTRATED BY CHRIS WORKMAN

IN COLLABORATION WITH JOSEF NEWGARDEN

FOR MY DAD AND BROTHER - WHO STARTED MY LOVE OF RACING OVER 30 YEARS AGO BY TAKING ME
TO MY FIRST INDY CAR RACE AT ROAD AMERICA - CW

THANKS TO MY PARENTS FOR ALL THE SACRIFICES THEY MADE, AND TO EVERY INDIVIDUAL THAT
HAD A HAND IN HELPING ME ACHIEVE MY RACING DREAMS! - JN

Published by Apex Legends, a division of Apex Communications Group, LLC. All text,
illustrations and design ©2016 Chris Workman and Apex Legends. All rights reserved.

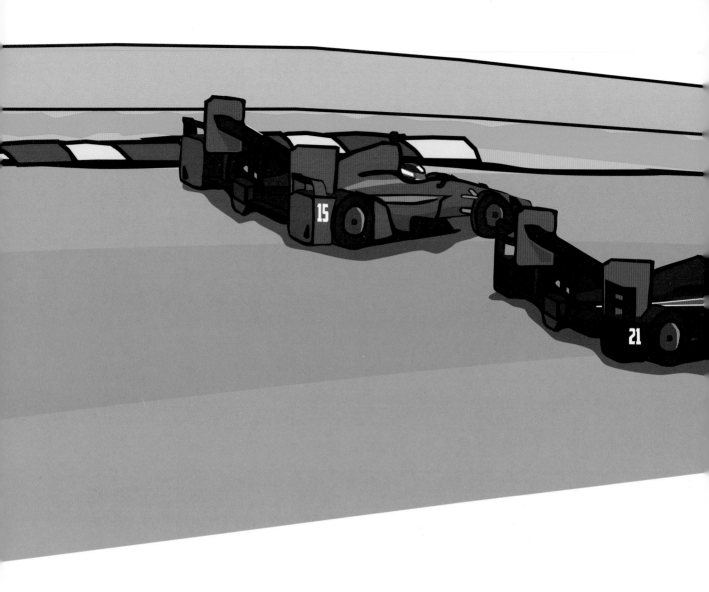

ACKNOWLEDGEMENTS

Thanks to the Indiegogo supporters and Josef Newgarden fans who contributed to this project through book pre-orders and information sharing, and to the media who have gotten behind this unique project. Without your help, this project would have never been possible!

Special thanks to Josef Newgarden, Leigh Diffey, Brian Bonner, Tom Moore and Bob Hillis for seeing the vision for this book and helping to make it a reality. Most importantly, thanks to my wife and kids for your ongoing patience and support!

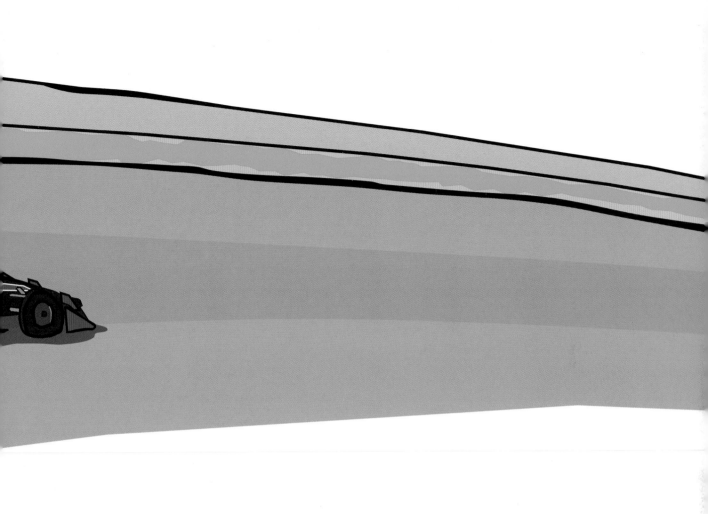

FOREWORD

It doesn't matter how old we become, there is always a small kid inside each of us. The compelling story of Josef the Indy Car Driver appealed to me because of the attraction Indy car racing has for children.

When I read bedtime stories to my two sons, I'm always listening to them, watching for their reactions; what grabs their attention, what opens their eyes wide, what holds them, what makes them laugh. Moreover, what ideas will they continue to discuss together, once the story is told and the book is closed.

Throughout childhood, certain events and experiences resonate with us, and these powerful memories remain influential for the remainder of our lives. In my capacity as a broadcaster, there's no question, when commentating any Verizon IndyCar Series race on television, I'm always hopeful that I'm not only explaining the thrilling on-track action to adults, but I want kids to be as excited as I am about this form of racing, I want to engage them, to inspire their imagination. We can never give children enough time, can never encourage them enough. And, we must never stop providing experiential learning.

Chris has done a truly elegant job, both with his text and his lovely illustrations, all depicting not only a day in the life of a committed and determined racer, but also revealing just how much a wonderfully memorable day at the race track can mean so much; with the reading of each page it all works beautifully to create that all important lasting impression.

- By Leigh Diffey, NBC Sports Commentator

Hi - I am Indy car driver Josef, Newgarden! If you aren't very familiar with Indy car racing I wanted to give you some quick information about the Verizon IndyCar Series before you dive into the story. **ENJOY!**

WELCOME TO INDY CAR RACING!

The Races: Each race I compete wheel-to-wheel against over twenty other drivers - Indy car racing is very competitive! Races are between 200 and 500 miles in length and require several pit stops to change tires and refuel the cars.

Pit Stops: Pit stops are really important - you could lose a race if you have a slow pit stop! That is why a great team and pit crew are an important part of winning.

Tracks: There are four types of racetracks in the Verizon IndyCar Series. I work with my team to make the car as fast as possible for each type of track.

The Championship: Drivers score points in each race based on how they finish. There are about fifteen races per season and whoever scores the most points is crowned series champion!

Winning races is the best way to become champion, however it is just as important that I finish every race.

LET'S LEARN ABOUT INDY CARS

Indy cars are some of the fastest cars on the planet! Their sleek design allows them to race at speeds up to 230 mph on superspeedway tracks.

The big tires are called "slicks." Their soft rubber helps the car grip the race track for super-fast cornering. The big wings mounted at the front and back keep the car on the track by working just like airplane wings... only upside down!

Indy cars don't have fenders - that is why they are called "open-wheeled." And, since there is only one seat in the open cockpit Indy cars are often called "single-seaters."

A turbocharged engine making up to 700 horsepower allows me to reach such high speeds - the acceleration is unbelievable! And, the huge brakes bring the car to a stop in a very short distance.

TYPES OF TRACKS

INDIANAPOLIS MOTOR SPEEDWAY
SUPERSPEEDWAY

PHOENIX INTERNATIONAL RACEWAY
OVAL

TORONTO
STREET CIRCUIT

ROAD AMERICA
PERMANENT ROAD COURSE

"SLICK" TIRES   BIG WINGS   SINGLE-SEATER   "OPEN-WHEELED"

It is a normal Saturday morning for Josef Newgarden. He is doing what he loves more than anything else...

DRIVING AN INDY CAR AS FAST AS POSSIBLE!

Josef and the rest of the Indy car drivers are practicing for the big race the following day.

After practice Josef talks to his crew chief about ways to make his car faster. He knows they can find more speed in his racecar!

Then he sees an old friend of his, Grandpa Jamie, looking at his racecar.

"Hi Josef! This is Cooper and Avery's first race and I was showing them around the paddock," Grandpa Jamie says. "Do you mind if we take a peek at your car?"

The crew has been working on the racecar so most of the bodywork has been removed. Josef teaches the kids about the Indy car.

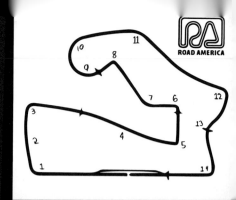

They learn how the **LARGE WINGS** at the front and back keep the cars pressed to the track ...

... how the **CHASSIS** is made up of the gearbox, engine and cockpit tub for added strength ...

... how the **TURBOCHARGED ENGINE** gives the car amazing speed ...

... how the **LARGE BRAKES** slow the car in less than the length of a football field ...

... and how the **BIG TIRE**
don't have tread so they ca
help the car turn faster!

osef explains that Road America is considered one of the greatest race tracks
ne world. While the track is fun to drive, he says it takes work to get the ca
etup right for the four mile long track's mix of **TIGHT CORNERS, LONG,
WEEPING TURNS** and **FLAT-OUT STRAIGHTS**.

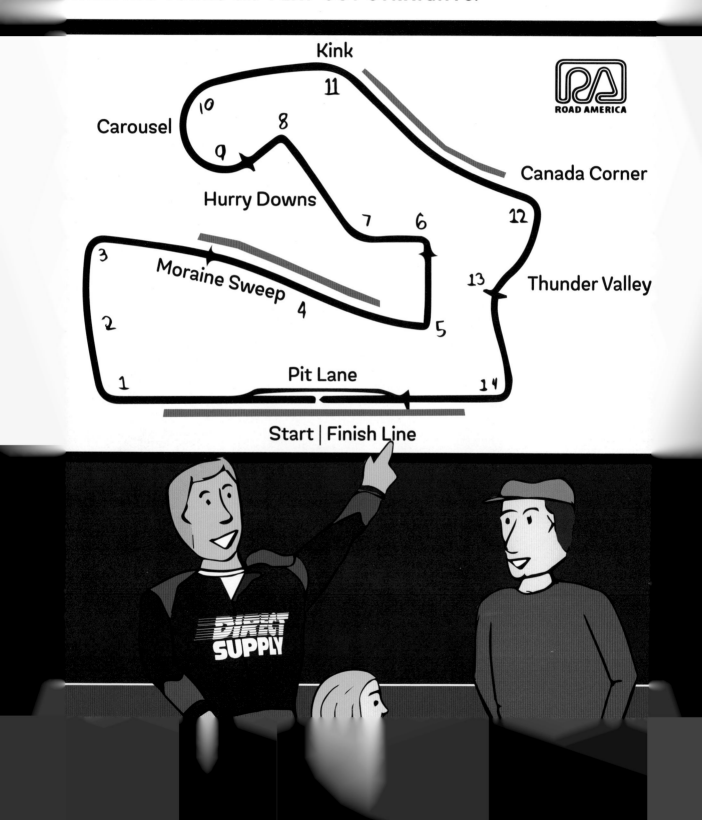

Then Josef shows them his favorite Indy car feature. "This little button on the steering wheel is called 'push-to-pass'. It gives me a **50 HORSEPOWER BOOST** to pass cars on the straightaways! I can only press it **TEN TIMES** per race so I have to use it wisely."

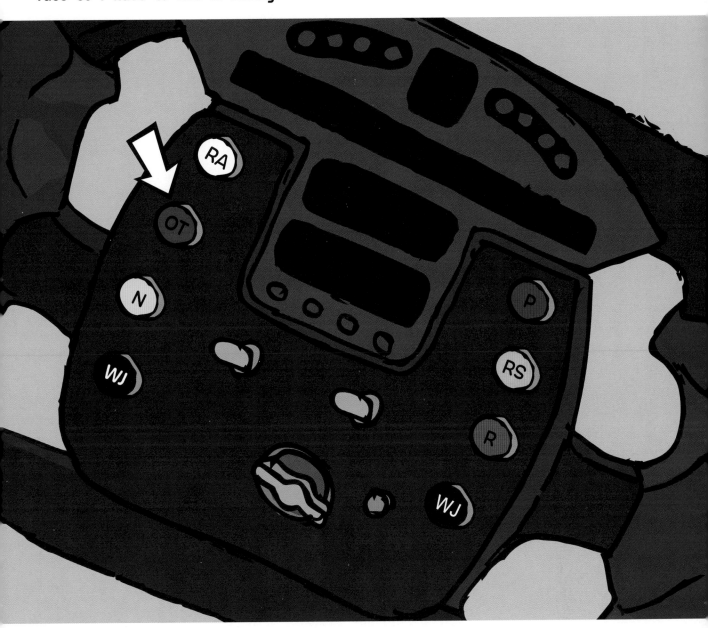

He tells them that the "push-to-pass" button will really come in handy on the three spots marked in red on the map.

Then Avery says, "I WANT TO BE AN INDY CAR DRIVER TOO. How did you get started?"

Josef tells the kids that his interest in racing began when he was around eleven years old.

But he didn't start in a racecar... his love of racing started on a **MOTORIZED SCOOTER!** Josef raced his friends up and down the street on his scooter.

Soon Josef switched to karting so he could learn to be a racecar driver.

"I LOVED KARTING!
I loved the speed ...

... I loved how fast the karts
turned corners ...

... and I LOVED the
competition," said Josef.

"I just knew racing is what I wanted to do with my life. So, I
started driving racecars after winning the karting championship."

The kids are amazed to hear about the different types of racecars Josef drove – each one **FASTER AND MORE CHALLENGING** than the last.

"After winning the Indy Lights Championship I moved up to the Verizon IndyCar Series," says Josef.

"It takes a lot of practice and hard work, but it is worth it to be able to drive one of the **FASTEST RACECARS** on the planet!

The best way to get started is to see if you like karting too!"

Then Grandpa Jaime asks, "How is the car running? Are you ready for tomorrow's race?"

"My car is running well - but we need to find more speed for qualifying." Josef wants to set a time that will get him as close to the front as possible!

That afternoon Josef tries to set the fastest lap he can in qualifying. After qualifying in 9th position, Josef knows the team needs to find a way to make his car faster through the turns if he is going to have a chance to win.

JOSEF WILL NEED TO PASS A LOT OF CARS IN THE RACE!

RACE QUALIFICATION ORDER

 2ND

  **1**ST (POLE)

4TH   **3**RD

6TH   **5**TH

8TH   **7**TH

10TH   **9**TH (JOSEF)

Race day morning is busy for Josef! He talks with TV reporters and meets guests.

Then in morning practice the team works on the car's setup and finds extra speed; **JOSEF IS HAPPY AND READY FOR THE RACE!**

IT IS ALMOST TIME FOR THE RACE! Everyone sings "The Star Spangled Banner". Then Josef climbs into his racecar after being introduced to the crowd.

Next, the announcer says the most famous words in racing: "Gentlemen, Start your engines!" After a short, **CLICK, CLICK, CLICK** the race engine fires to life with a loud **VRRROOOOOOMMMMMMM!**

The pace car leads the pack as the cars warm up to make sure they are safe to race.

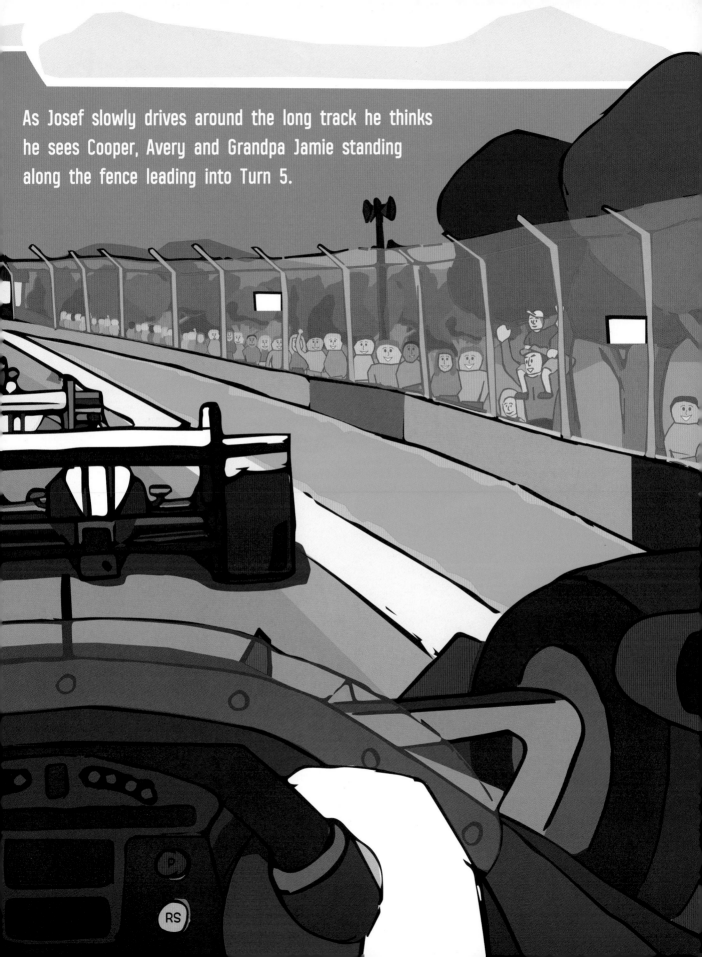

As Josef slowly drives around the long track he thinks he sees Cooper, Avery and Grandpa Jamie standing along the fence leading into Turn 5.

The pace car pulls into pit lane and
the green flag waves to start the race. With a
**SOUND MORE FEROCIOUS THAN THOUSANDS OF
ANGRY HORNETS,** twenty-four racecars scream up the Front Straight!

With his newly found speed, Josef passes several cars during the first few laps!

Cooper, Avery and Grandpa Jamie watch the cars brake hard, turn and head up the hill towards turn 6. **SUDDENLY A CAR SPINS ON THE TRACK!**

Josef loses a few spots as he swerves to avoid hitting the car.

Over the next few laps Josef focuses on catching the race leaders. He pushes his car to the limit and regains several positions. Josef has moved up to sixth position when his crew chief radios that his car needs fuel and tires.

THE NEXT LAP JOSEF PULLS INTO PIT LANE. His pit crew hurries to get him back into the race, but he loses a few positions.

It is about halfway through the race and Josef has worked his way back up to sixth position. He has closed in on the fifth place car and is fighting hard to make a pass!

Josef knows **HE MUST GET BY** if he is going to be able to catch the leaders.

Josef sees his chance to make a pass as both cars speed through Hurry Downs towards the Carousel.

HE DIVES TO THE INSIDE as they enter the long turn. The other driver isn't giving up as they speed through the Kink!

Two laps later both drivers are racing hard and closing in quickly on fourth place! Josef presses **"PUSH-TO-PASS"** as he rockets up the Front Straight.

He squeezes inside of his opponent just in time to **SLAM ON HIS BRAKES** to make the pass into Turn 1!

SUDDENLY THERE IS A CRASH! Two cars are out of the race after colliding and hitting the tire barrier.

Corner workers wave yellow flags to slow the cars down so track safety crews can clean up the mess and make sure everyone is OK.

IT IS BUSY ON PIT LANE - all the cars are making their final pit stops.

Josef's pit crew is lightning fast - THEY ADD FUEL AND
CHANGE TIRES IN UNDER EIGHT SECONDS!

The speedy pit stop allows Josef to stay in fourth place; he is ready
for the sprint to the finish!

The green flag drops to restart the race! Josef works hard to defend his position. **HE HAS TO STAY IN FRONT IF HE WANTS A SHOT AT WINNING!**

Josef catches up to the third place car after several fast laps. He makes a tough pass going through Thunder Valley with only three laps to go!

Cooper and Avery see the pass and jump up and down with excitement!

IS IT POSSIBLE FOR JOSEF TO CATCH THE LEADER AND WIN?

There are only two laps to go! Josef is chasing first and second place through the Carousel turn.

HE BLASTS FLAT-OUT THROUGH THE WOODS and catches up to the silver car heading into Canada Corner.

Josef slams on the brakes at the last possible moment and makes the pass!

The white flag waves as Josef crosses the start-finish line behind the lead car.

THERE IS ONLY ONE LAP TO GO AND THE FANS ARE ON THEIR FEET!

Josef tries to pass the leader into the first turn but can't get by. He refuses to give up, and closes back in to set up another pass.

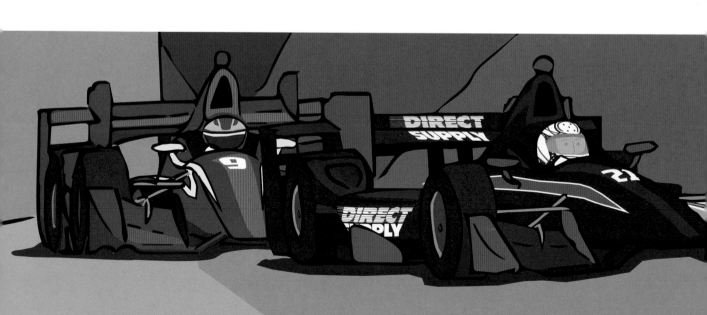

Josef is inches away from his opponent through Turn 5. Then he swerves inside as they climb the hill and makes a tough pass into Turn 6!

COOPER, AVERY AND GRANDPA JAMIE SEE
THE PASS AND LET OUT A ROARING CHEER!

Everyone is watching closely to see if Josef can hold on to the lead. There are several lapped cars that need to be passed and second place is right on his tail!

Josef's opponent tries to make a pass in the last turn, but Josef is able to hold him off and **TAKE THE CHECKERED FLAG FOR THE WIN!**

Winning the race puts Josef in third place in the championship with only a few races to go in the Verizon IndyCar Series season!

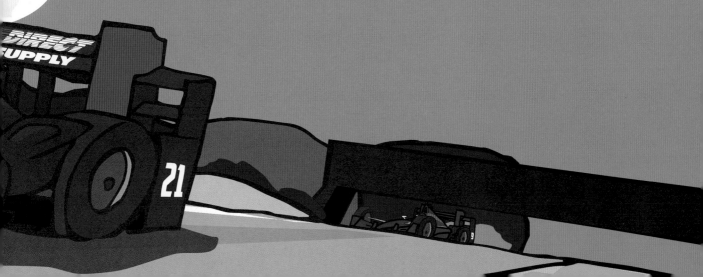

After completing a victory lap he celebrates in Victory Lane with his team!

Avery, Cooper and Grandpa Jaime join the rest of the crowd in Victory Lane. They are excited their new hero won the race!

Several weeks later Josef is surprised when he receives a letter from some of his newest fans!

Hi Josef -

Congratulations on your amazing win at Road America!
Thank you for taking the time to teach us about racing
and what it is like to be an Indy Car driver.

Your story has inspired us to try karting! Here are
pictures from our first time at the track. Avery even won
one of her races!

Your friends,
Cooper, Avery and Grandpa Jamie

DO YOU WANT TO BE AN INDY CAR DRIVER TOO?

I hope this story has encouraged you to learn more about Verizon IndyCar Series racing. You should try watching a race on TV or better yet, go to a track!

If going 200 mph down the front straight of a track like Road America is your dream, here are some important things you can do now to prepare to be a racecar driver.

EAT RIGHT & EXERCISE

Did you know that most drivers sweat so much during a race that they lose over 5 pounds in weight? When I race my heart rate stays around 180 beats per minute over the entire 2-3 hour race!

That level of effort is about the same as a marathon runner or long-distance cyclist, so it is very important that you stay in good shape & eat the right foods.

JOSEF'S RACING CAREER TIMELINE

2003 - 2006	2006 - 2008	2008 - 2009
KARTING	**SKIP BARBER**	**FORMULA FORD**
Two Karting Championship (2006)	Southern Region (2006)	Formula Ford Festival Winner (2008)
	6th National Championship (2007)	2nd British Formula Ford Championship (2009)
	2nd National Champinoship (2008)	

STUDY HARD

While racing requires a great deal of physical activity, it requires even more thought! Learning science – especially math & physics – helps you to understand how to work with your race crew to make the car go faster. Writing and speaking skills are vital to working with your team, sponsors and the media.

And, since you may end up racing in another country, knowing a foreign language is useful too! Most importantly, learn to think through problems... because in every race you will face many unknown challenges!

TRY DRIVING AND SEE IF YOU REALLY LIKE IT

Racing video games are a great way to begin driving real racecars. But, to really get a sense of driving, go to a go-kart track. Once you are old enough, an indoor karting center is the best bet to get a taste for actual racing!

STAY POSITIVE – you can do it! I hope to see you at the track!

It all started in 2003 karting... and less than 10 years later I was racing an Indy car in the Indy 500!

2010	2011	2012 - PRESENT
GP3	**INDY LIGHTS**	**VERIZON INDYCAR SERIES**
European FIA GP3 Series	1st Indy Lights Championship	Wins at Barber Motorsports Park & Toronto *
		* as of printing